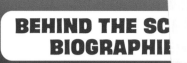
BEHIND THE SC
BIOGRAPHIE

T0011418

WHAT YOU NEVER KNEW ABOUT

>>>———————————<<<

TIMOTHÉE
CHALAMET

by Dr. Nafeesah Allen

CAPSTONE PRESS
a capstone imprint

This is an unauthorized biography.

Spark is published by Capstone Press, an imprint of Capstone
1710 Roe Crest Drive, North Mankato, Minnesota 56003
capstonepub.com

Copyright © 2024 by Capstone. All rights reserved. No part of this publication may be reproduced in whole or in part, or stored in a retrieval system, or transmitted in any form or by any means, electronic, mechanical, photocopying, recording, or otherwise, without written permission of the publisher.

Library of Congress Cataloging-in-Publication Data
Names: Allen, Nafeesah, author.
Title: What you never knew about Timothée Chalamet / by Dr. Nafeesah Allen.
Description: North Mankato, Minnesota : Capstone Press, [2023] | Series: Behind the scenes biographies | Includes bibliographical references and index. | Audience: Ages 9 to 11 | Audience: Grades 4-6 | Summary: "Timothée Chalamet has taken Hollywood by storm. He has dazzled on both the big and small screens. But what is his life like when the cameras aren't rolling? High-interest details and bold photos of his exciting life will enthrall reluctant and struggling readers, while carefully levelled text will leave them feeling confident"— Provided by publisher.
Identifiers: LCCN 2022058762 (print) | LCCN 2022058763 (ebook) | ISBN 781669049487 (hardcover) | ISBN 9781669049302 (paperback) | ISBN 9781669049319 (pdf) | ISBN 9781669049333 (kindle edition) | ISBN 9781669049340 (epub)
Subjects: LCSH: Chalamet, Timothée—Juvenile literature. | Motion picture actors and actresses—Biography—Juvenile literature. | LCGFT: Biographies.
Classification: LCC PN2287.C467 A3 2023 (print) | LCC PN2287.C467 (ebook) | DDC 791.4302/8092—dc23/eng/20221222
LC record available at https://lccn.loc.gov/2022058762
LC ebook record available at https://lccn.loc.gov/2022058763

Editorial Credits
Editor: Mandy Robbins; Designer: Heidi Thompson; Media Researcher: Jo Miller; Production Specialist: Tori Abraham

Image Credits
Alamy: Abaca Press, 6, Album, 14, BFA, 24, Entertainment Pictures, 11, Moviestore Collection Ltd, 25, 26, PictureLux / The Hollywood Archive, 16, Richard Levine, 12; AP Photo/Jason DeCrow, File, 9, Getty Images: Albert L. Ortega, 8, Andreas Rentz, 18, Chung Sung-Jun, 21, Lia Toby, 29, Pascal Le Segretain, 19 (right), 23, Tim P. Whitby, Cover, 17, 27 (bottom), Vittorio Zunino Celotto, 19 (left), Newscom: Aria Isadora/Guest of a Guest/Si, 10; Shutterstock: Alona_S, 27 (top), Beskova Ekaterina, 7, FocusStocker, 5, Fred Duval, 4, Ihor Pasternak, 20, Kathy Hutchins, 13 (middle), Oleksii Arseniuk, 21 (background), Ron Adar, 13 (bottom), s bukley, 13 (top), Tupungato, 13 (background)

All internet sites appearing in back matter were available and accurate when this book was sent to press.

Printed and bound in China. PO5379

TABLE OF CONTENTS

Words in **bold** are in the glossary.

ACTOR, ICON, ATHLETE?

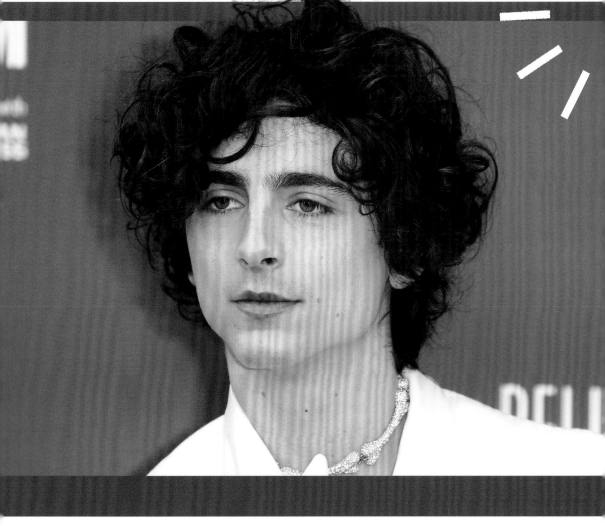

Timothée Chalamet is a serious actor. He's a fashion **icon**. But did you know he started out in TV ads? He thought they were fun, but he really wanted to be a soccer star when he grew up.

What else might surprise you about this famous actor? Find out!

GROWING UP
CHALAMET

Timothée, his parents, and his sister, Pauline

Because of his name, most people think Timothée is French. He's not, but his father is. His mother is Jewish American. Timothée was born in New York City.

The Chalamet family spent summers in France. Timothée speaks the French language **fluently**.

Timothée has some famous family members. His sister, Pauline, acts and writes. His aunt Amy Lippman co-created the 1990s TV show *Party of Five*.

Amy Lippman

Timothée loves bringing his family to award shows. He brought his parents and sister to the Oscars in 2018!

HIGH SCHOOL,
MUSICAL

Timothée thought acting in commercials was just for fun. He didn't take acting seriously until he saw *The Dark Knight*. Heath Ledger impressed him as the Joker. When it was time for high school, Timothée applied to LaGuardia High School for Music and Performing Arts.

LaGuardia High School for Music and Performing Arts

Lots of big names went to this famous New York City high school. Nicki Minaj, Al Pacino, and Jennifer Aniston are a few. Bad grades almost kept Timothée out. But his **audition** was so impressive, the theater teacher made sure he got in.

Al Pacino

Nicki Minaj

Jennifer Aniston

13

SPECIAL
SKILLS

Elle Fanning and Timothée on the set of *A Rainy Day in New York*

Every actor has special skills. Speaking French is just one of Timothée's. He also plays piano, guitar, and chess. In high school, he even started rapping.

Can you guess his rapper names? They were "Lil' Timmy Tim" and "Timmy T." He once made a rap about his **statistics** teacher.

FACT
Timothée learned Italian for his role as Elio in *Call Me By Your Name*.

FAMOUS FRIENDS

Timothée's friends call him Timmy.
He has some famous pals. He was in several
movies with his good friend Saoirse Ronan.
They met while working on *Lady Bird*.

Saoirse Ronan

Timothée went to school with Ansel Elgort and Madonna's daughter Lourdes Leon. He is friends with Pete Davidson, Selena Gomez, and Zendaya too.

Zendaya

FASHION
FAVORITE

Timothée enjoys expressing himself through clothes. Instead of having a stylist, he likes to dress himself for award shows. Timothée loves making unique choices. His style led him to be the first man on the cover of *British Vogue*.

CHALAMET
BY THE NUMBERS

Looking for some stats on Timothée Chalamet? He was born December 27, 1995. (He doesn't like having a birthday two days after Christmas.) Timmy was just 17 when he started studying at Columbia University.

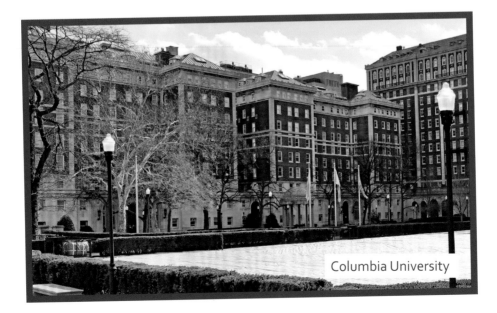

Columbia University

What about his height? It's 5 foot, 10 inches.

6' — 6'

5'9" — 5'9"

5'6" — 5'6"

5'3" — 5'3"

5' — 5'

4'9" — 4'9"

4'

S.R. STUDIO. LA.CA.

What about Timmy's social media numbers?
Timothée has a TikTok page with about
154,000 followers. He posts on Twitter too.
Around 2 million people follow him there.
He has about 18 million Instagram followers
as well. His first post was in 2014. It was of
two birds snuggling on his balcony.

WIN SOME,
LOSE SOME

Timothée has wowed fans with his acting skills. His performances in *Little Women* and *Dune* were impressive. He was **nominated** for an Oscar for his role in *Call Me By Your Name*. But he has missed out on plenty of roles too.

Did you know Timothée tried out to be Spider-Man? Could you imagine Timmy as Peter Parker instead of Tom Holland? What other movies did Timothée not make the cut for? *The Theory of Everything* and *Miss Peregrine's Home for Peculiar Children.*

Tom Holland as Spider-Man

POP QUIZ!

Have you been surprised by any Timmy trivia yet? See if you can pass this celeb pop quiz.

1. What position did little Timmy play on his middle school basketball team?

2. What show was his first on-screen role?

3. What is his favorite snack?

4. What is his favorite type of music?

FACT
During the filming of *Little Women*, Timmy and the rest of the cast were spied snacking on Wendy's french fries.

1. Trick question-he was the mascot **2.** *Law & Order*
3. French Fries **4.** Hip-hop

Glossary

audition (aw-DISH-uhn)—a tryout performance for an actor or musician

fluent (FLOO-uhnt)—able to easily speak a language

icon (EYE-kon)—someone who is honored and respected

nominate (NOM-uh-nate)—to name someone as a candidate for an award or job

statistics (stuh-TISS-tiks)—the science of collecting numerical facts, such as a baseball player's achievements on the field

Read More

Allen, Nafeesah. *What You Never Knew About Zendaya.* North Mankato, MN: Capstone Press, 2024.

Andral, Dolores. *What You Never Knew About Selena Gomez.* North Mankato, MN: Capstone Press, 2023.

Ware, Lesley. *How to Be a Fashion Designer.* New York: DK Penguin Random House, 2018.

Internet Sites

Every Upcoming Timothée Chalamet Movie
screenrant.com/timothee-chalamet-movies-future-upcoming/

Timothée Chalamet
imdb.com/name/nm3154303/

Timothée Chalamet Biography
biography.com/actor/timothee-chalamet

Index

About the Author

Dr. Nafeesah Allen is a world traveler, wife, and mom of two. Her family speaks English, Spanish, and Portuguese, and has surprise dance parties in the kitchen.